JAPAN

Bryan E. Coates

With photographs by Jimmy Holmes

The Bookwright Press
New York · 1991

Our Country

Australia
Canada
China
France
Greece
India
Italy
Japan
Pakistan
The Soviet Union
Spain
The United Kingdom
West Germany

Cover *A view of Mount Fuji seen across rice paddies.*

First published in the
United States in 1991 by
The Bookwright Press
387 Park Avenue South
New York, NY 10016

First published in 1991 by
Wayland (Publishers) Limited
61 Western Road, Hove
East Sussex, BN3 1JD, England

Library of Congress Cataloging-in-Publication Data
Coates, Bryan E. (Bryan Ellis)
  Japan/Bryan Coates.
    p. cm. — (Our country)
  Includes bibliographical references and index.
  Summary: An introduction to the people, places, foods, industries,
customs, and agriculture of Japan.
  ISBN 0-531-18392-0
  1. Japan—Juvenile literature. [1. Japan.] I. Title.
II. Series: Our country (New York, N.Y.)   90-25053
DS806.C66 1991   CIP
952—dc20   AC

Typeset by Dorchester Typesetting Group Limited
Printed in Italy by Rotolito Lombardo S.p.A.

All words printed in **bold** are explained in the glossary on page 30.

Contents

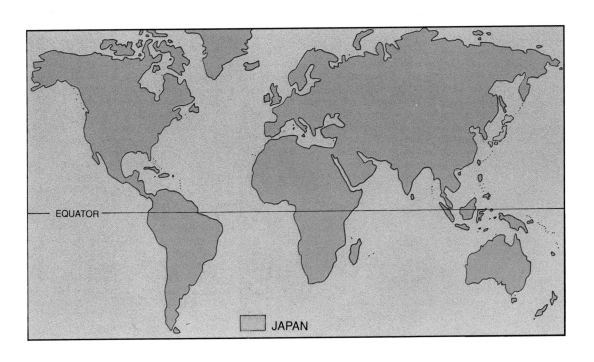

EQUATOR

JAPAN

We live in Japan

Japan is a country in the Pacific Ocean. It consists of many islands – the four biggest are Hokkaido, Honshu, Kyushu and Shikoku. Across the Sea of Japan the nearest countries are Korea, China and the USSR. Far away across the Pacific Ocean are the United States and Canada.

Japan's **capital** is Tokyo. It is a very rich and crowded city. The emperors of Japan used to live in Kyoto, which was the capital for a thousand years, but now the Emperor lives in Tokyo.

Japan is a land of mountains and fast-flowing rivers. There are many **volcanoes**. Sometimes there are **earthquakes**, and **typhoons** and **tidal waves** sweep in from the Pacific Ocean.

The Golden Temple at Kyoto. This beautiful pavilion was built for a nobleman, about 600 years ago.

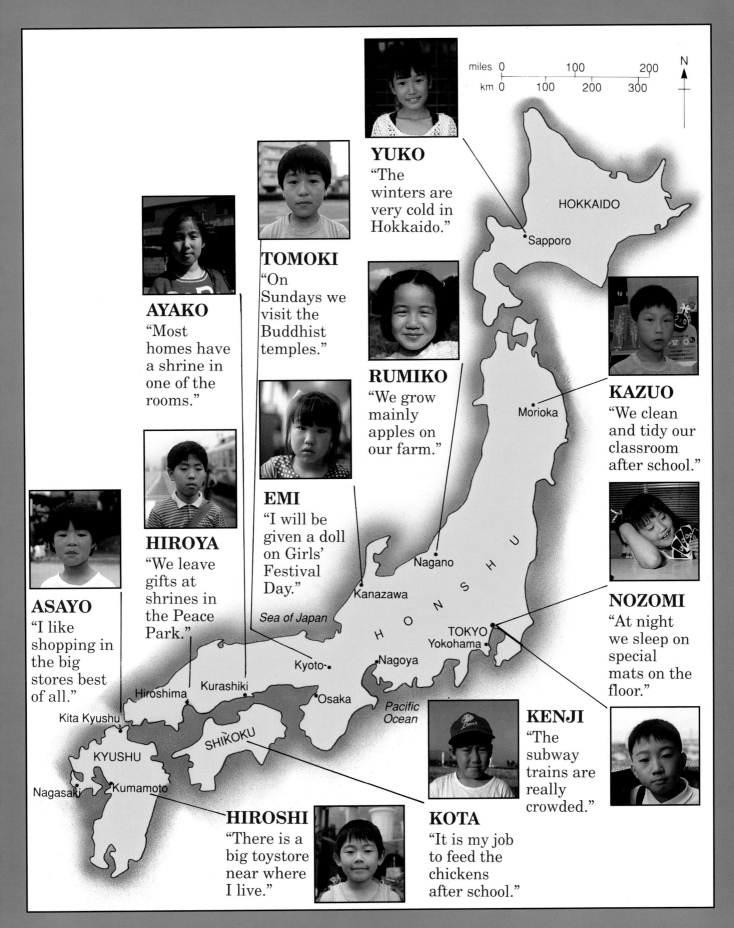

YUKO
"The winters are very cold in Hokkaido."

TOMOKI
"On Sundays we visit the Buddhist temples."

AYAKO
"Most homes have a shrine in one of the rooms."

RUMIKO
"We grow mainly apples on our farm."

KAZUO
"We clean and tidy our classroom after school."

EMI
"I will be given a doll on Girls' Festival Day."

HIROYA
"We leave gifts at shrines in the Peace Park."

NOZOMI
"At night we sleep on special mats on the floor."

ASAYO
"I like shopping in the big stores best of all."

KENJI
"The subway trains are really crowded."

HIROSHI
"There is a big toystore near where I live."

KOTA
"It is my job to feed the chickens after school."

miles 0 · 100 · 200
km 0 · 100 · 200 · 300

N

HOKKAIDO

Sapporo

Morioka

HONSHU

Nagano

Kanazawa

Sea of Japan

TOKYO
Yokohama

Kyoto

Nagoya

Osaka

Pacific Ocean

Hiroshima · Kurashiki

Kita Kyushu

SHIKOKU

KYUSHU

Nagasaki · Kumamoto

The weather

The Japanese are very aware of the different seasons of the year. As the seasons change the Japanese eat different foods, wear different clothes and decorate their houses with different flowers and pictures.

The weather is very varied. In Hokkaido the winters are long and very cold and the summers are short and warm. In Kyushu the winters are very mild and the summers

A snow-covered beach on Hokkaido, Japan's most northerly island, where the winters are very cold.

are hot and **humid**. Northwest Honshu
has very deep snow and the trees are often
supported by poles to help them carry the
weight of snow.

The south is very wet. When a typhoon
crosses Japan, huge amounts of rain fall in
a few hours. September is the most
dangerous month for typhons.

"We take umbrellas everywhere!"

"I am Yuko, and my big sister is
Sayoko. We live in Hokkaido,
which is the island in the far
north of Japan. Here, the
winters are very cold and we
have a lot of snow and ice. It
also rains a lot and we often
need our umbrellas."

"We have strong winds in the typhoon season."

"My name is Emi, and I live in
Kanazawa, on the coast of the
Sea of Japan. In the typhoon
season we have very strong
winds. In our local park all the
trees are supported by big
poles. These keep the trees
from being blown down."

Fishing and farming

Women planting rice. One is using a small planting machine and the other is putting the seedlings in by hand.

The Japanese eat mainly fish, rice and vegetables. They catch more fish than anyone else in the world. The seas around Japan are rich in fish of many kinds. Tuna is very popular, as is octopus. The long coastline is dotted with fishing ports, and the fish markets are exciting places to visit.

The coastal plains and lower mountain slopes are farmed. The land is **irrigated** and **terraced.** Rice is the most important crop. It is grown in flooded fields called rice **paddies**.

Oranges, peaches, apples and **satsumas** are also grown. Bags are often tied over the

8

"In spring the countryside is very beautiful."

"My name is Rumiko. My father and mother are farmers. We grow mainly apples, and we also have some rice fields. In the spring the land is covered with little lakes, as the small rice paddies are prepared for the new seedlings."

"I like to feed the chickens."

"My name is Kota. I live in Shikoku, which is a farming area. We used to grow rice but now we grow barley instead. We also have chickens and my job is to feed them after school. My father shares a **harvester** with some of the other farmers. Here I am riding on the harvester."

fruits to protect them. Flowers, especially chrysanthemums, are grown in greenhouses.

All sorts of different vegetables are grown, often under plastic sheets for protection. In the supermarkets and vegetable stand you would notice the huge white radishes.

Industry and jobs

After World War II ended, in 1945, Japan was very poor. But the people worked hard to build up their industries, and now Japan is a rich and powerful country. It produces huge amounts of iron and steel, and many cars, ships and **electronic products**. But it has to **import** many necessary materials such as **iron ore**, oil, coal, cotton and wool.

Most countries in the world now want to buy Japanese products, and many Japanese names are very well known, such as Toyota,

Putting the finishing touches to cars on the assembly line at a Nissan car factory.

"My father drives a truck."

"My name is Ayako, and I live in Kurashiki. My father is a truck driver. He collects and delivers goods all over the western part of Japan. He works every day except Sunday. Here I am sitting in the cab of his truck."

"This robot can draw cartoons."

"My name is Asayo, and I live with my mother in Kitakyushu, in the south of Japan. My uncle works in a factory where they make **robots**. Here I am in his workshop, watching a robot that has been programmed to draw cartoons. Robots are sold to places like car factories."

Mazda, Honda, Panasonic, Sony, Hitachi and Nissan.

There are not many people in Japan without a job. Most work in banks, stores, schools, hospitals and transportation services. But not all workers are highly trained or well paid.

Schools

Schoolchildren hard at work in the classroom.

Education is very important to the Japanese. Children start school at the age of 6 and most stay until they are 18. They work very hard and many go on to college after completing twelve years in their elementary, middle and high schools.

School is from 8:30 a.m. to 4:30 p.m., and on Saturday mornings. Japanese children are good at math, and they also have to learn to read **Kanji** (Japanese script), which is very difficult and takes many years. Many children take extra lessons in the evenings and on Saturday afternoons, because they want to pass their exams.

School uniforms are worn by all school-children. All high school boys and girls wear the same dark blue or black school uniforms. Children carry book bags on their backs and travel on their own to school by bus, train and subway.

"I have to pass my school tests."

"My name is Hiroya, and I live in Hiroshima. I go to a **cramming school** on some evenings because I have to pass my tests to get into Junior High School. The work is very hard. I travel by train, which is always very crowded."

"Going over the bars is great fun."

"My name is Kazuo, and I live in Morioka. I enjoy exercising in the school playground. I like math, but I don't much like learning *Kanji* because it is very difficult. We always clean and tidy our classroom before we go home. We try not to make a mess so that it won't take us too long."

Religion

The interior of a Buddhist temple.

There are many religions in Japan. The most important are **Shinto** and **Buddhism**. Shinto is unique to Japan. Shinto **shrines** are everywhere; their *torii* wooden gateways are very striking. Shinto belief is that nature itself is sacred, and Shintoists believe there are gods everywhere – in trees, mountains, rivers and rocks.

A Japanese person would probably be **baptized** and married in a Shinto shrine but buried in a Buddhist temple, because the Buddha is thought to look after the

"Kyoto is famous for its shrines and temples."

"My name is Tomoki, and I live in Kyoto. On Sundays we visit some of the great temples in Kyoto. This is a Buddhist temple. Buddhism is a very important religion in Japan."

"There is a shrine in most Japanese homes."

"My name is Ayako. This is the shrine in our home. It is in a corner of the living room. Most Japanese homes have a shrine in one of the rooms. This shrine is to keep good luck in the home and it is where we pay our respects to our ancestors."

dying and the dead. All traditional homes have a Buddhist shrine where members of the family pay respects to their **ancestors**.

Kyoto, the old capital city of Japan, has more than a thousand Shinto shrines and Buddhist temples.

15

Festivals

Most Japanese would say that religion is not very important in their lives. But they still hold traditional values and they still go to the local shrine festivals, especially the great New Year's celebrations and the summer *Bon* festival to remember the dead.

Japan is a land of festivals and national holidays. Every village has its festivals when the rice is planted and harvested. Some towns have their own very famous festivals.

The third days of the third month is Girls' Festival, when girls dress in beautiful **kimonos**. They display beautiful dolls dressed in traditional costumes in their

New Year's pilgrims at Fushima Inara Shrine, Kyoto. This is one of the most famous Shinto shrines in Japan.

"My grandmother is giving me a doll on Girls' Day."

"I am Emi. On March 3rd we celebrate a girls' festival. On this day Japanese girls are given very beautiful dolls. The dolls are all set out in special stores before the festival. This year my grandmother is buying me a festival doll."

"Origami cranes are symbols of peace."

"I am Hiroya. This is the Peace Park in Hiroshima. We leave gifts at shrines in the park, to remember all the people who died in the **atomic bomb** blast in August 1945. Today I have brought **origami cranes** made of paper to this special shrine, to celebrate peace and to remember all the children who died."

homes. The fifth day of the fifth month is Children's Day, when boys tie huge decorated paper **carps** to poles in the garden or attached to the house.

Homes

Many Japanese houses are still built of wood in the traditional way.

About half the people in Japan live in overcrowded cities. Land is very scarce and expensive and homes are often small. Few have yards. Many people live in rented apartments in high-rise buildings called *danshi*, located at the edges of the cities. Homes are bigger in the **suburbs**, but the daily journey to work may take as much as two hours each way in very crowded trains.

Houses in the countryside are much larger. They are built of wood. Most have to be built on little islands standing above the flooded rice fields.

Many houses have thick straw mats called *tatami* on the floor. At night thin mattresses are unrolled on the *tatami* to sleep on.

18

Instead of inside walls, there are very light sliding doors that can be taken out to make the rooms larger.

"The walls in our house are like sliding doors."

"I am Nozomi. I live in a suburb of Tokyo. I am lucky because where I live there is plenty of space. In the center of Tokyo people have to live in small apartments. In our house we sit or kneel on chairs that have no legs, and we sleep on *tatami* mats on the floor. In the daytime our bedding is stored in cupboards."

"My grandparents live next door."

"My name is Hiroshi, and I live in Kumamoto. Our house was built in the usual way, from modern light-weight materials. But my grandparents' house, which is next to ours, is made of **prefabricated units** and it was put up in just two days. Here I am with my grandfather, outside his house."

Leisure

The Japanese work hard and play hard. They enjoy playing baseball, and watching it on TV. They also like to play golf. In the winter lots of people go to the Japanese Alps for skiing and other winter sports. The **traditional** sports of **sumo** wrestling, **judo**, kendo (fencing), **karate** and kyodo (archery) are still very popular.

Although the Japanese enjoy going to theaters and movies, the three classical forms of drama – *Noh* and *Bunraku* (puppet dramas) and *Kabuki* (traditional drama) –

Sumo wrestling is a very popular sport in Japan. The huge wrestlers struggle to push each other out of the ring.

are still very popular and watched by many people.

Many Japanese people now take vacations abroad. But in their own country the **hot-springs resorts** are still the favorite places for most older people. These resorts are found throughout the country.

"I am learning kendo."

"I am Kota. After school I go to my kendo class. Kendo is like fencing, only we use bamboo swords instead of metal ones. My grandmother lives with us and she helps me to get my equipment ready. It is really uncomfortable to wear all these thick clothes when the weather is hot."

"Japanese chess is quite difficult."

"I am Yuko. Sometimes, during the long winter evenings here in Hokkaido, my sister Sayoko and I play Japanese chess. Although it's fun to play it's quite a difficult game. Sayoko usually beats me!"

Food

The Japanese-style breakfast often consists of soup, rice and raw egg, dried fish and pickled vegetables. Green tea (not black) is drunk with the meal. Some people now eat Western-style breakfasts.

The main meal is in the evening. It normally consists of several dishes. As many as thirty items of food may be served. A lot of fish, vegetables and rice is eaten. Fish is often eaten raw and must be very fresh. Chopsticks are used rather than knives and forks.

Food changes with the seasons. *Sukiyaki* and *shabu shabu* are meat and vegetable dishes cooked in a big pot at the table. They

A stand selling all kinds of colorful vegetables.

"I like hamburgers and French fries."

"I am Kazuo. Sometimes we go to a fast-food place. It is difficult to park nearby because there are so many cars in the towns. I like to eat hamburgers and French fries from McDonalds, but I'm not allowed to have them very often."

"Traditional Japanese cooking is best."

"I am Nozomi. Although I like to eat hamburgers sometimes, I like my mother's cooking best. She cooks traditional Japanese food – lots of different dishes with fish, vegetables and rice. It's delicious!"

are eaten in the colder months. Summer iced drinks are splendidly refreshing.

The type of food eaten varies from region to region. For instance, Nagoya specializes in noodles, and Kyoto is famous for its traditional cooking.

Shopping

Crowds of shoppers in the Ginza on a Sunday afternoon, when this famous shopping street in Tokyo is closed to traffic.

The Japanese love shopping. The main shopping centers in the cities are often built around busy railroad stations. Even small towns have **arcades** of stores in or near the station. Because the stores are near the stations, they are convenient for many shoppers coming to town from the country. Shopping centers have also been built below ground.

In Tokyo, the three main railroad stations are all centers for many of the best department stores in the world, as well as other exciting shops and restaurants.

Tokyo's most famous shopping street is the Ginza, which is full of huge department stores and other small traditional shops. It is closed to traffic of Sunday afternoons, which is the busiest shopping time for many Japanese families.

"In this store they let me try things out."

"I am Asayo. I like the cake shop because they let me pick what I want and take it to the counter. But best of all I like shopping in the big stores. In the television and stereo department they let me use the electronic handset."

"This is a very good toystore."

"I am Hiroshi. There is a big toystore near where I live. They sell lots of small toys, and kites, quite cheaply. I sometimes go to the supermarket with my mother. But I like to shop there only if I can choose what we buy. I like fish, so the fish counter is where we go first."

Transportation

The world famous Bullet Train (*Shinkansen*) runs from Tokyo to towns in the north and west of the country. I takes ten hours to travel from one end of the bullet train line to the other. Like all trains in Japan it is always on time. Other trains are often very crowded and uncomfortable, especially in the hot and humid summers.

Most roads, too, are crowded and travel times are slow. But many families do not have a car. They prefer to rely on trains, buses and taxis. Almost everyone uses a bicycle at times.

Japan's seaports are very busy, with lots of ships carrying oil, coal and manufactured foods to and from the country.

There are a great many cars in Japan, and many city streets have been rebuilt to cope with the increasing numbers.

Because Japan is such a long country, many people like to travel by air. There are airports in all big cities. JAL and ANA are the biggest airlines.

"It's easy to get lost in the subway."

"I am Kenji. We don't have a car because we live in the middle of Tokyo. My father says there are far too many cars in Tokyo. I usually travel by train. The subway trains are really crowded, and I sometimes think I could easily get stuck among the passengers and not be able to get off!"

"The *Shinkansen* is one of the fastest trains in the world."

"I am Kazuo, My father and I are going on the *Shinkansen* or Bullet Train. It costs a lot, but it goes very fast – it goes at 150 mph (240 kph) all the way to Tokyo. I'm very excited to be traveling on it."

Let's discuss Japan

If you look around you at home, at school, in your town or village you will see a lot of things that were made in Japan. You will soon notice Japanese cars such as Toyota, Nissan and Mazda; motorcycles made by Honda and Kawasaki; and TV sets, videos, radios and calculators. Perhaps you have also seen Japanese-run factories near where you live.

Sometimes sumo wrestlers appear on TV. Adults and children from Western countries often study judo or karate.

Facts

Population: 123 million
Capital: Tokyo
Language: Japanese
Money: Japanese yen
Religion: Shinto and Buddhism

A natural hot spring gushing out of the ground in a volcanic region of the Japanese Alps.

The Tea Ceremony, an ancient Japanese tradition, when tea is served to guests in a special way and in a special room.

Japan is different in many ways from this country. Look carefully at the pictures in this book. Decide what you would like to talk about to the Japanese children who have been telling you about their country. Think what you would tell them about *your* country.

Glossary

Ancestors   People far back in a family and no longer alive, such as great grandparents and their parents, grandparents and so on.

Arcade   A covered street lined with stores and restaurants.

Atomic bomb   A very powerful bomb used in World War II. One was dropped on Hiroshima on August 6, 1945, and another on Nagaski three days later. Both cities are in Japan.

Baptized   Received into a religious group by being sprinkled with water in a special ceremony.

Buddha   Gautama Buddha was a teacher who lived from about 563 to 483 BC.

Buddhism   The religion built on the teaching of the Buddha.

Capital   The city where the government of a country is based.

Carp   A colorful fish in lakes, streams and garden ponds all over Japan. On May 5, painted paper carps flutter outside homes where there are boys, because the carps is the symbol of courage.

Cramming school   A school open in the evenings and on weekends to give extra classes to pupils preparing for exams.

Crane   A large, long-necked wading bird that is a symbol in Japan of happiness and beauty.

Earthquake   Earth tremors resulting from intense pressures in the Earth's crust.

Electronic products   Products such as radios, TVs, videos and calculators based on the use of tiny electronic "chips."

Harvester   A machine for cutting and gathering in an agricultural crop such as wheat or rice.

Hot-springs resorts   Places where naturally hot water gushes out of the ground. The water contains healing minerals, and people go there to bathe.

Humid   Moist. Humid air makes one feel uncomfortably hot and sticky.

Import   To bring goods in from another country.

Iron ore   Rock containing iron.

Irrigated   Supplied with water to grow crops. Dry land must be irrigated to grow plants.

Judo   A form of wrestling.

Kanji   Japanese symbols or characters.

Karate   The art of hitting or jabbing an opponent with the fists or feet.

Kimono   A long, sashed robe with wide sleeves.

Origami   Japanese art of folding paper into all kinds of shapes, perhaps a crane, frog or flower.

Paddies Irrigated fields where rice is grown.

Prefabricated units Sections built in a factory and brought to the building site ready for assembly.

Robots Machines programmed to do jobs instead of human beings.

Satsuma A type of mandarin orange, native to Japan.

Shinto The religion of Japan. It is a religion based on a belief that nature is peopled by spirits.

Shrines Places of worship.

Suburbs The areas where people live on the outskirts of large towns and cities.

Sumo An ancient sport of wrestling fought by huge men.

Terraced When hillsides are cut into steps so that irrigated paddies or vegetable plots can be formed on the leveled ground.

Tidal wave An unusually high wave that causes great damage. It is usually set off by an earthquake out at sea.

Traditional Following old ways, customs and practices.

Typhoon A violent storm with strong winds and heavy rain. It can cause a great deal of damage.

Volcano A mountain with a crater from which molten rock, ash or steam is sometimes thrown out.

Books to read

Downer, Lesley. *Japan*. New York: Bookwright Press, 1989.

Jacobsen, Peter and Preben Kristensen. *A Family in Japan*. New York: Bookwright Press, 1984.

Moon, Bernice, and Cliff Moon. *Japan Is My Country*. New York: Bookwright Press, 1985.

Steele Anne. *A Samurai Warrior*. New York: Bookwright Press, 1986.

Tames Richard. *Japan: The Land and Its People*. New York: Hampstead Press, 1986.

Picture acknowledgments

All photographs by Jimmy Holmes except the following: Eye Ubiquitous pages 16, 18, 29; Geoff Howard 6; Tony Stone *cover*, 24; ZEFA 20. Maps on contents page and page 5 are by Jenny Hughes.

Index